Cultures of the World!
USA, Canada & Mexico
Culture for Kids
Children's Cultural Studies Books

PROFESSOR GUSTO
EDUCATIONAL & INFORMATIVE BOOKS FOR CHILDREN
(PRE-K / K-12)

Learning the culture of a country can help us understand its people. It can guide us as we interact with them.

Knowing other cultures is a meaningful step towards achieving peace and unity.

American Culture

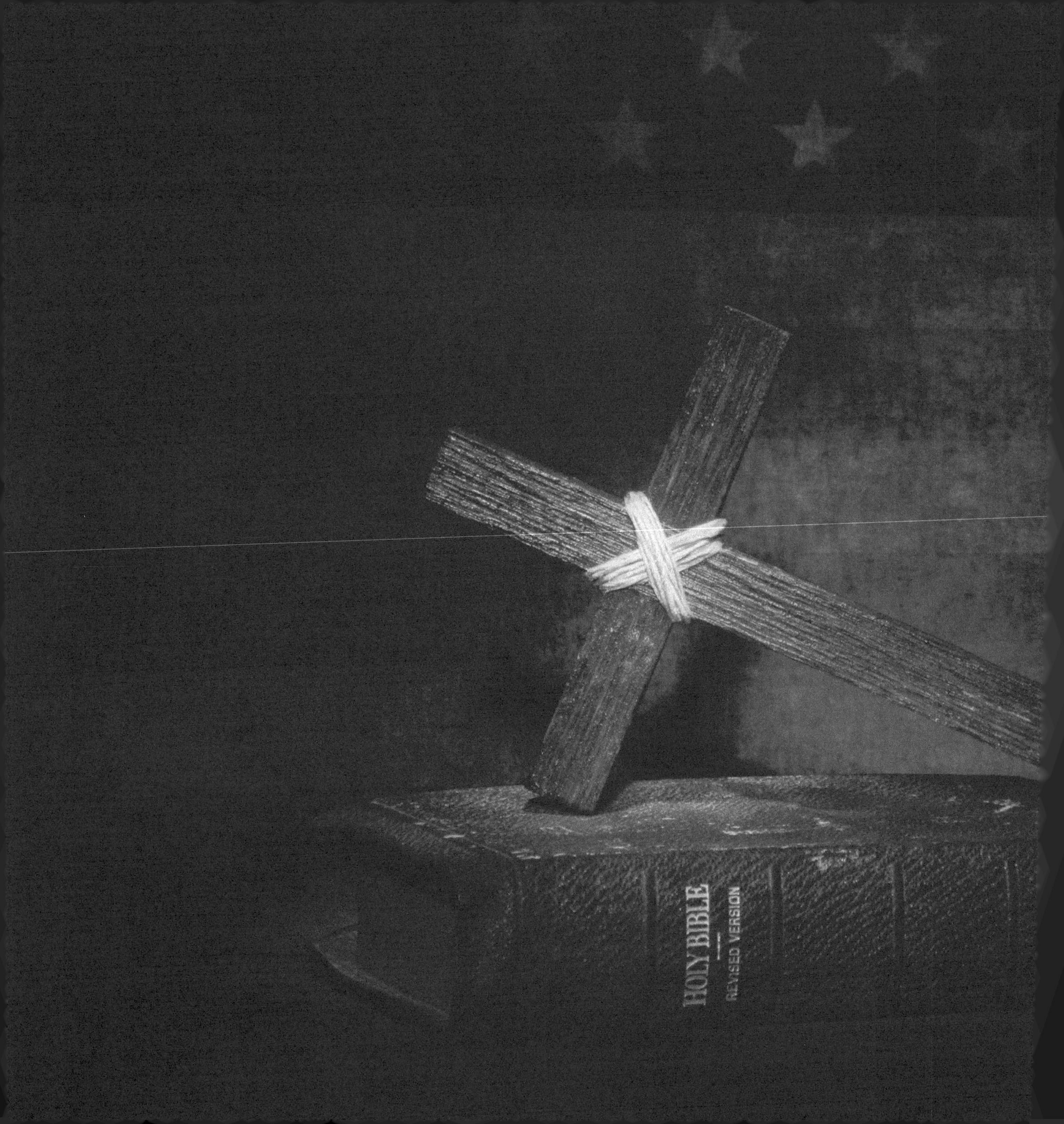
HOLY BIBLE
REVISED VERSION

In the United States, people follow nearly every known religion, but 83% of its population are Christians. The second highest religious affiliation is Judaism.

Clothing styles vary. It depends on social status, occupation, climate and region. Some distinctive items of clothing are blue jeans, running shoes, baseball caps and boots. American celebrities and the media have greatly influenced the fashion around the world.

The United States combines European and Native American influences. Hamburgers, potato chips, macaroni and cheese, and pizza are just few examples of food identified as American.

America's national sports are baseball and football. Being a sports minded country, the US follows football, baseball, hockey, basketball and other sports.

Canadian Culture

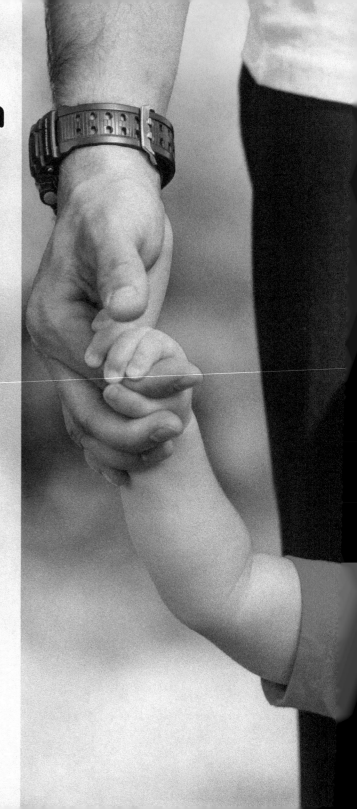

A typical Canadian family is not easy to define because Canadians come from many different racial and religious backgrounds. The majority of its population are Catholics and Protestants.

When Canadians are introduced, it is their custom to shake hands. A light touch or tap on the shoulder during discussion is also common. But when greeting friends, Canadians do not often kiss or hug.

Canadians are often casual at home. Don't get offended if your visit does not include a formal meal and entertainment. While in their homes, most Canadians do not wear hats or their outdoors shoes.

NO SMOKING
within **20** metres
of the Sporting Area
and any Spectator Area

Ontario

SMOKE
FREE
ONTARIO

Smoking is not permitted in most public buildings in Canada. Hence, smoking has become less popular. Most Canadian families don't allow smoking in their homes.

Mexican Culture

In business and family matters, Mexicans put a high value on hierarchy and structure. Mexican families are typically large. They have a close relationship with their relatives and they are mindful of their responsibilities to their family members and close friends.

Mexicans love to host parties. They are known to entertain their visitors well. This is an important part of Mexican values and customs.

Income level and social class play an important part in Mexican culinary norms. Working class Mexicans love to eat corn or wheat tortillas with beans, tomatoes and chorizo. Hot, spicy foods are common among Mexicans.

Mexico is known for its well-developed beverage industry, especially for their tequila. This is made from agave cactus. Mexicans also love soda.

Cultural awareness is important. It helps us understand one another. Some cultures have greatly influenced others, and this helps draw people together.

There is more
to know about
the culture
of the USA,
Canada
and Mexico.
Research and
have fun!

CPSIA information can be obtained
at www.ICGtesting.com
Printed in the USA
LVHW06s1250080518
576285LV00043B/46/P

9 781683 219965